Shelley Rotner &
Stephen Calcagnino

Photographs by Shelley Rotner

ORCHARD BOOKS
NEW YORK

THE BODY BOOK

Orchard Books, A Grolier Company, 95 Madison Avenue, New York, NY 10016

Manufactured in the United States of America. Printed and bound by Phoenix Color Corp.
Book design by Mina Greenstein. The text of this book is set in 29 point Futura Medium.
10 9 8 7 6 5 4 3 2 1

Library of Congress Cataloging-in-Publication Data
Rotner, Shelley. The body book / by Shelley Rotner and Steve Calcagnino. p. cm. Summary: Simple text and
photographs present some of the parts of the human body, including eyes, nose, hands, legs, and toes.
ISBN 0-531-30256-3.—ISBN 0-531-33256-X (lib. bdg.)
1. Body, Human Juvenile literature. [1. Body, Human.]
I. Calcagnino, Steve. II. Title. QM27.R676   2000   611—dc21   99-34866

To everyone who shares my life
—S.R.

To Helen and Tony
—S.C.

We all have bodies with many different parts.

We have eyes to see,

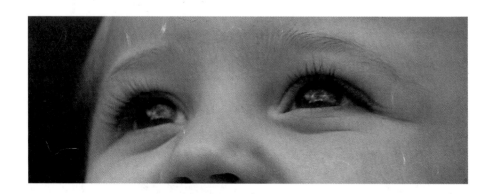

a nose to smell,

ears to hear and a mouth to talk,

tongues
to taste,

teeth to bite and chew.

Hands to touch,

arms to hug and hold,

legs and feet
to run and jump,

elbows and knees
to bend and move.

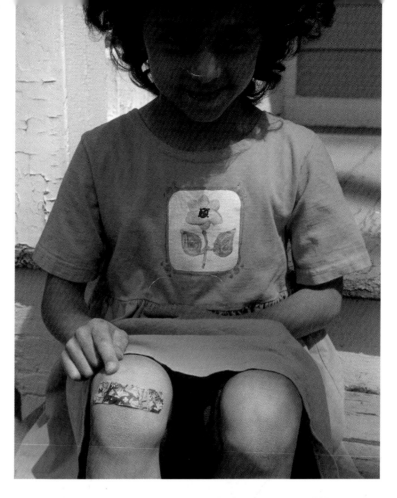

Fingers,
toes,

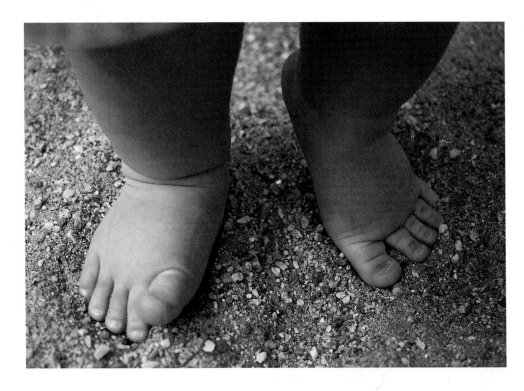

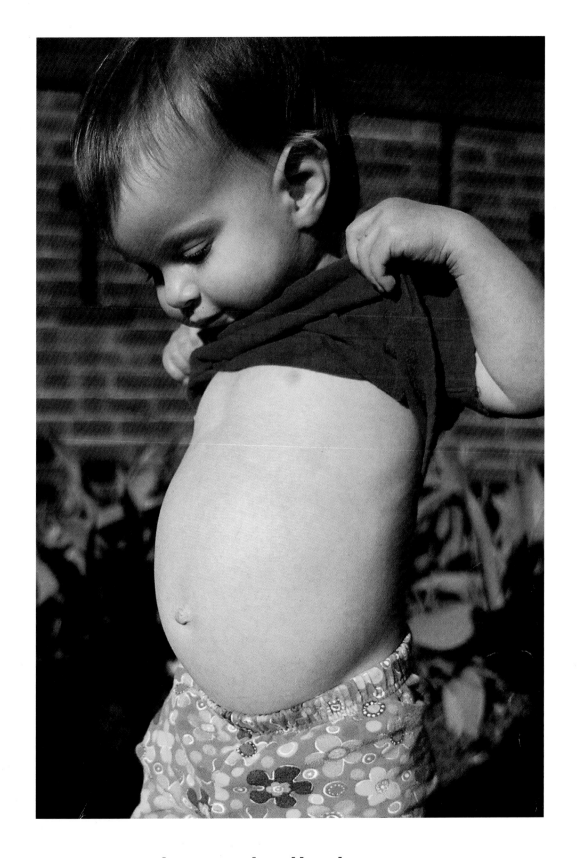

and one belly button.

Our bodies can
do many things.

Young, old,

big, small.

Bodies!
All shapes, colors,
and sizes.